Let's Make a

Pasta Salad

by Mari Bolte

NORWOOD HOUSE  PRESS

Norwood House Press

For information regarding Norwood House Press, please visit our website at:
www.norwoodhousepress.com or call 866-565-2900.

PHOTO CREDITS: page 4: ©Charles Brutlag / Shutterstock; page 7: ©Pav-Pro Photography Ltd / Shutterstock; page 8: ©dabyki.
nadya / Shutterstock; page 11: ©Rosa Herrara / ; page 12: ©Drazen Zigic / Shutterstock; page 15: ©kungverylucky / Shutterstock;
page 16: ©Rimma Bondarenko / Shutterstock; page 19: ©Rosa Herrara; page 21: ©Rosa Herrara; page 22: ©Rosa Herrara; page
23: ©Rosa Herrara; page 24: ©Rosa Herrara; page 27: ©Rosa Herrara; page 28: ©Rosa Herrara

© 2023 by Norwood House Press.

Hardcover ISBN: 978-1-68450-780-1
Paperback ISBN: 978-1-68404-751-2

LIBRARY OF CONGRESS CATALOGING-IN-PUBLICATION DATA

Library of Congress Cataloging-in-Publication Data has been filed and is available at catalog.loc.gov

353N—082022
Manufactured in the United States of America in North Mankato, Minnesota.

Contents

CHAPTER 1

All about Pasta Salad 5

CHAPTER 2

Making Pasta Salad 13

CHAPTER 3

In the Kitchen! 20

Glossary 30
For More Information 31
Index 32
About the Author 32

Pasta salad is the perfect side dish or main meal.

All about Pasta Salad

Nothing is better than a big bowl of pasta. And when you add dressing, it can be shared as a salad!

Pasta salad is usually served cold. It can be as simple as pasta tossed with salad dressing or mayonnaise. Vegetables, meat, or other yummy ingredients can be added. If it's something you find delicious, you can probably add it to pasta salad!

People have been eating pasta for a long time. The Chinese made noodles thousands of years ago. Scientists found proof of this in 2005 when a sealed bowl of noodles was found. It was buried 10 feet (3 meters) under the ground. The long, thin noodles were made from **millet**. The millet had been ground into flour. Next, the flour was turned into a dough that was stretched and pulled. Then, the noodles were cooked while fresh. The 4,000-year-old noodles that were found were perfectly **preserved**.

People in the Middle East were probably the first people to dry pasta. They used **durum** wheat, which is sturdy and dries well. Couscous and acini di pepe are little pearl-shaped bits of pasta. They are easy to store and cook quickly in hot water. The ancient Arabs were probably the first to make long noodles like spaghetti and vermicelli too.

Chinese noodles are hand-pulled by twisting, stretching, and folding.

Durum did not reach Italy until much later. But once it did, it became very popular. Most dried pasta today uses durum wheat. It is ground into a flour called semolina. Semolina is used to make pasta, bread, and pizza dough.

An extruder pushes pasta dough through a disk. Different disks shape pasta into a variety of shapes.

Art showing Italian people making pasta dates back to the 4th century BCE. That's around 2,400 years ago! Southern Italy has good growing weather. Italians began tossing pasta with olive oil and the vegetables that grew there.

At first, pasta was simple—noodles and flat sheets. But soon, they were being rolled, cut, and folded into shapes. By the 1600s, **extruder** machines pushed out dough in different shapes, such as elbow macaroni. These machines also made it faster and easier to make and sell noodles. In the 1700s, Europeans finally realized forks were useful tools for picking up noodles. Before, they mostly used their hands.

Future president Thomas Jefferson ate pasta when he was in Europe in the 1780s. He was interested in how it was made. Jefferson asked a friend to buy him a pasta machine. Back in America, his chefs made him macaroni!

During the late 1800s, large numbers of Italian **immigrants** made new homes in America. They brought their pasta recipes with them. People quickly learned that pasta was easy to prepare. It was also delicious!

The love of pasta stretched across the globe. In Hawaii in the 1880s, pineapple and sugar **plantation** workers needed a quick and delicious lunch to eat in the middle of the day.

Not everyone brought their own food. Food carts would sell premade lunches. A simple salad of macaroni, mayonnaise, salt, and pepper became a popular side dish. Mayonnaise is a simple combination of eggs, vinegar, and oil. Today, Hawaii's macaroni salad is still part of affordable and tasty plate lunches.

In the 1950s, the restaurant Trattoria da Vincenzo in Capri, Italy, changed the game. They made the first official pasta salad. This salad had tomatoes, mozzarella, basil, and pasta dressed in olive oil. It was the perfect light meal.

Parts of a Pasta Salad

Meat

Cheese

Vegetables

Dressing

Pasta

CHAPTER 2

Gluten-free pasta noodles are great for all sorts of recipes!

Making Pasta Salad

Most pasta uses durum wheat. It is ground into semolina flour. The flour has a **protein** called gluten. The gluten gives it a firm, chewy bite. It also keeps **starch** in the pasta from **leaching** into the water.

Gluten-free pasta is made with other flours, though. Corn and rice are the two most common. Chickpeas and lentils are others. Starchy things, such as potatoes or **xanthan gum**, are added to copy the texture of regular pasta.

Gluten is why pasta doesn't just stick together in a clump when added to water. Higher protein means the pasta will be more likely to hold its shape and texture when boiled.

Pasta is best cooked in salted water. Noodles don't have much flavor on their own. Salt makes them taste better. It makes food taste sweeter and less bitter. That is why a pinch of salt is always added to baked goods. Pasta water should be very salty. Add 1 to 2 tablespoons of salt per box of pasta.

If you start pasta in cold water, the salt won't be dissolved enough to help flavor the noodles. Add the noodles once the water is boiling. The pasta will soak up some of that salt as it cooks. Boiling the water also makes sure the pasta cooks evenly.

Starch from the noodles makes pasta water white and cloudy.

When you drop the pasta into the pot, give the water a stir. During the first stage of cooking, the starch in the pasta bursts. It is released into the water. Dried pasta is full of rigid starch. When cooked, the starch can swell into a sticky gel.

Most salad dressings are emulsions. They are mixtures of two things that usually don't combine, like oil and water.

It's important not to overcook pasta. When boiled for too long, the molecules break down. The proteins no longer hold things together. The pasta goes from a rigid shape to a floppy blob.

Draining the pasta when it's still firm, or **al dente**, is important. When making a pasta salad, rinse the noodles in cold water. This stops the cooking process. It also washes away the starchy coating that can make the pasta stick together.

After the pasta is cooked, a dressing can be added. Vinaigrettes are mixtures of vinegar, oil, pepper, and salt. Sometimes, sugar is added. Vinegar is water-based. It doesn't mix well with oil. But try whisking or shaking. This motion allows them to mix enough to be tossed in a salad.

Mayonnaise is a vinaigrette with egg yolks added. The yolks have a type of fat called lecithin. This helps water and oil mix.

Once your salad is dressed, it's time to decide what else to add. Meats like shredded chicken, ham, diced sausage, or tuna fish are full of healthy proteins. Vegetables like carrots, cucumbers, olives, or zucchini can be sliced and diced. Grilling is a way to get even more flavor. The high heat toasts the sugars in the foods. That makes veggies sweeter.

Cheese is a great source of **calcium**. Calcium helps your body build strong bones. Choose from crumbly, creamy, hard, shredded, or diced cheese. Leafy greens like lettuce, spinach, or arugula have healthy vitamins and **nutrients**. They make a pasta salad healthier. Pasta salads with greens look fresh and add crunch.

Fruit can be added to pasta salad too. It can taste nice with tangy vinegar. Nuts are another good choice. They are full of protein. They also add a nice crunchy texture.

Materials Checklist

✓ cutting board, sharp knife, and mixing spoon

✓ vegetables, such as bell pepper, cucumber, red onion, tomato, and black olives

✓ cheese or dairy-free alternative

✓ pepperoni or salami (optional)

✓ 1 pound dry shaped pasta, such as macaroni, spirals, or gluten-free

✓ mixing bowl and large pot

✓ colander

✓ 2 cups Italian dressing

✓ salt and pepper

Always have an adult help when using the stove or sharp knives.

CHAPTER 3

In the Kitchen!

Now that you've had time to think about pasta salad, it's time to make some! Start with a simple Italian pasta salad.

1. With an adult's help, use the cutting board and knife to prep the vegetables, cheese, and meat. Slice and dice into bite-sized pieces, then set aside.

2. With an adult's help, read the instructions on the package of pasta. It will tell you how much water to use and how long to cook the pasta. Don't forget to add salt to the water for added taste!

Always be careful around boiling water and have an adult there to help.

3. Heat the pot of salted water until it boils.

4. Once the water is boiling, cook the pasta to al dente.

5. With an adult's help, drain the cooked pasta in a colander. Rinse with cold water. Drain well.

6. Pour the pasta into a large bowl.

24

7. Toss with the Italian dressing.

8. Add the vegetables, cheese, and meat if using.

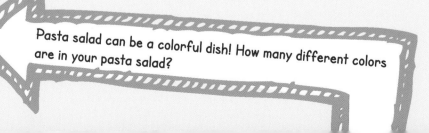
Pasta salad can be a colorful dish! How many different colors are in your pasta salad?

9. Toss the salad well until everything is evenly mixed.

10. Cover the bowl and refrigerate the pasta salad for 1 hour.

11. Give it a taste! Season with salt and pepper, if desired. Then, serve it!

Decide what you like best about your dish. Over time, you'll develop a pasta salad full of all your favorite flavors!

Dressing Up Your Salad

Congratulations! You have made a pasta salad. Now see if there are ways to make it even better. Use any of these changes and see how they improve your pasta salad.

- For a creamy salad, replace up to half of the Italian dressing with mayonnaise.

- Layer pasta salad ingredients in a jar with a lid, starting with the vinaigrette. Pack the jar for on-the-go eating. When it's time for lunch, just shake the jar and everything will mix together.

- Experiment with the ingredients. Remove any you don't like. Add your favorites instead. Try a different kind of meat or cheese. Try a different kind of dressing, such as ranch or Asian, or make your own vinaigrette.

Glossary

al dente (al DEN-tay): cooked but still firm

calcium (KAL-see-um): a mineral needed for healthy teeth, bones, and bodies

durum (DUR-uhm): a type of wheat used to make dried pasta; when ground into flour, durum is called semolina

extruder (ek-STROOD-uhr): a machine that shapes materials by pushing them through a hole

immigrants (IM-uh-gruhntz): people who move to another country

leaching (leech-ING): draining away

millet (MIL-uht): a cereal plant used to make flour

nutrients (NOO-tree-yunts): substances found in food that give the body energy and good health

plantation (plan-TAY-shuhn): land where crops such as coffee or sugar are grown

preserved (pruh-ZURVD): prepared in a way that keeps something from decaying

protein (PRO-teen): a molecule that is present in all living things; protein in food is part of a healthy diet

starch (STARCH): a carbohydrate found in grains and potatoes; starch is white, but odorless and tasteless

xanthan gum (ZAN-than GUM): a food additive used to help gluten-free food hold its shape

For More Information

Books

Hunt, Santana. *Making Salads with Math!* New York, NY: Gareth Stevens Publishing, 2020.

Knutson, Julie. *Macaroni and Cheese: An Out-of-the Box Story*. Ann Arbor, MI: Cherry Lake Publishing Group, 2022.

Loh-Hagan, Virginia. *Weird Science: Food*. Ann Arbor, MI: Cherry Lake Publishing Group, 2022.

Websites

Barilla: How It's Made: Pasta's Journey from Farm to Table (https://www.youtube.com/watch?v=VYC0Wonk4a4) How is pasta made? This video shows you how.

Britannica Kids (https://kids.britannica.com/students/article/pasta/276298} Kids learn about the history of pasta and how it's made.

The Kitchen Pantry Scientist: The Science of Emulsions: Vinaigrette and Mayonnaise (https://kitchenpantryscientist.com/emulsions-mayonnaise-and-vinaigrette/) Learn how to make a delicious vinaigrette and a foolproof mayonnaise.

Index

cooking, 15, 17

dressing, 5, 17
dried pasta, 7, 15

extruders, 9

history, 6–7

instructions, 20–28

materials checklist, 19

plate lunch, 10

salt, 10, 14, 17
shapes, 6, 9, 14, 16
starch, 13, 15, 17

Trattoria da Vincenzo, 10

About the Author

Mari Bolte has worked in publishing as a writer and editor for more than 15 years. She has written dozens of books about things like science and craft projects, historical figures and events, and pop culture. She lives in Minnesota.